Unveiling the Weaknesses: An Analysis of the World Health Organization's COVID-19 Response

ROBERTO MIGUEL RODRIGUEZ

Copyright Page

TITLE: Unveiling the Weaknesses: An Analysis of the World Health Organization's COVID-19 Response

1ST Edition

ISBN: 9798223157915

Table of Contents

Unveiling the Weaknesses: An analysis of the World Trade Organization's COVID-19 Response

By Roberto Miguel Rodriguez

In this analysis, we will delve deeper into the weaknesses that have plagued the World Health Organization (WHO) in its handling of the COVID-19 pandemic. It is crucial to understand these shortcomings in order to improve future global health responses and ensure better outcomes for all.

One of the key weaknesses of the WHO's COVID-19 response has been the lack of transparency in its decision-making process. This has raised concerns among politicians, diplomats, journalists, educators, and the public. Without clear and open communication, trust in the organization's actions and recommendations can be undermined.

Another notable weakness has been the inconsistent messaging and communication with the public. Mixed signals and contradictory information have caused confusion and hindered effective public health measures. This has resulted in a reduced ability to control the spread of the virus and protect communities.

The delayed response and slow action in implementing measures have also been significant weaknesses of the WHO. Timely and decisive action is crucial in containing infectious diseases, yet the organization has been criticized for its sluggish response, leading to a rapid spread of the virus and an increased death toll.

Furthermore, the WHO has faced criticism for its failure to effectively coordinate and collaborate with other international health organizations. The lack of a cohesive global response has hindered efforts to control the pandemic and share vital information and resources.

Insufficient allocation of resources and funding has further hampered the WHO's ability to respond effectively to the crisis. Developing countries have been particularly impacted, as the organization has struggled to provide adequate support for their healthcare systems.

The mental health impact of the pandemic has also been neglected by the WHO. As the world grapples with the physical consequences of the virus, the psychological toll on individuals and communities must not be overlooked.

Additionally, the organization has faced criticism for its inability to address and mitigate the economic consequences of the pandemic. A comprehensive approach to the crisis should include strategies to support businesses, workers, and economies.

Moreover, the limited focus on vulnerable populations and marginalized communities has been a significant weakness. These groups often face unique challenges and require targeted interventions to ensure their well-being and safety.

Lastly, criticisms of bias and politicization within the organization's handling of the pandemic have further eroded public trust. It is essential that the WHO maintains its independence and prioritizes public health over political considerations.

In conclusion, the weaknesses in the World Health Organization's COVID-19 response have been multi-faceted and have had far-reaching consequences. By acknowledging and addressing these shortcomings, we can strive for a more robust and effective global health system that is better equipped to handle future pandemics.

Chapter 1: Introduction

Background on the COVID-19 pandemic

The COVID-19 pandemic has undoubtedly been a global crisis of unprecedented proportions. As the world grapples with the devastating impact of the virus, it has become increasingly clear that the weaknesses in the World Health Organization's (WHO) response have had far-reaching consequences. This subchapter aims to provide a comprehensive background on the COVID-19 pandemic and shed light on the various shortcomings of the WHO in addressing this crisis.

One of the key weaknesses of the WHO's handling of the pandemic has been the lack of transparency in its decision-making process. The public has often been left in the dark regarding the rationale behind certain measures and guidelines, leading to confusion and mistrust. This lack of transparency has further been exacerbated by inconsistent messaging and communication with the public. Mixed messages and contradictory information have eroded public confidence and hindered the effectiveness of public health interventions.

Another glaring weakness has been the delayed response and slow action in implementing necessary measures. Time is of the essence in a pandemic, and the WHO's failure to act swiftly has cost lives. Moreover, the organization has struggled to effectively coordinate and collaborate with other international health organizations, leading to fragmented and disjointed efforts to tackle the pandemic.

Insufficient allocation of resources and funding has also hampered the WHO's response. The organization has been unable to adequately support healthcare systems in developing countries, where the impact of the pandemic has been particularly severe. This lack of support has further exacerbated existing inequalities in global health.

Additionally, the WHO has overlooked the mental health impact of the pandemic. The psychological toll of the crisis has been immense, yet the organization has failed to prioritize mental health and provide adequate support to those affected.

Furthermore, the WHO has been criticized for its inability to address and mitigate the economic consequences of the pandemic. The global economy has suffered a severe blow, and the organization's limited focus on vulnerable populations and marginalized communities has perpetuated existing inequalities.

Criticisms of bias and politicization within the organization's handling of the pandemic have also emerged. Accusations of favoritism and undue influence have cast a shadow on the WHO's credibility and impartiality.

In conclusion, the COVID-19 pandemic has exposed several weaknesses in the WHO's response. From the lack of transparency and inconsistent messaging to the delayed response and insufficient allocation of resources, these shortcomings have had profound consequences. It is imperative for politicians, diplomats, journalists, educators, and the public to critically analyze the weaknesses of the WHO's handling of the pandemic in order to learn from these mistakes and ensure a more effective response to future crises.

Significance of analyzing the World Health Organization's response

The COVID-19 pandemic has exposed various weaknesses in the World Health Organization's (WHO) response, raising concerns among politicians, diplomats, journalists, educators, and the general public. Analyzing the WHO's response holds great significance as it sheds light on the shortcomings that need to be addressed to better handle future health crises. This subchapter will discuss the critical areas where the WHO's response fell short, emphasizing the need for improvement.

One of the primary weaknesses of the WHO's handling of the pandemic was the lack of transparency in the decision-making process. Many decisions and guidelines were implemented without clear explanations, leaving room for doubt and mistrust. This lack of transparency eroded public confidence in the organization and hindered the global response to the crisis.

Inconsistent messaging and communication with the public further exacerbated the situation. Mixed messages from the WHO confused both policymakers and the general public, leading to a lack of clarity in implementing preventive measures. This inconsistency eroded trust in the organization's ability to provide accurate information and guidance during a crisis.

Another significant weakness was the delayed response and slow action in implementing necessary measures. The WHO's hesitancy in declaring a global health emergency and providing timely guidance hindered countries' ability to respond effectively. The consequences of this delay were devastating, resulting in the rapid spread of the virus and loss of lives.

The failure to effectively coordinate and collaborate with other international health organizations also highlighted a weakness in the WHO's response. Global health crises require a united front, but the WHO struggled to effectively collaborate and coordinate efforts with other organizations, leading to fragmented responses and duplication of efforts.

Insufficient allocation of resources and funding further hampered the WHO's response. The organization lacked the necessary resources to effectively address the pandemic, resulting in limited testing capabilities, inadequate medical supplies, and insufficient support for healthcare systems in developing countries.

Moreover, the WHO neglected the mental health impact of the pandemic, focusing primarily on physical health. The psychological toll of the crisis on individuals and communities was largely overlooked, highlighting a failure to provide comprehensive support during a time of heightened anxiety and stress.

Furthermore, the inability to address and mitigate the economic consequences of the pandemic showcased another weakness. The WHO's response primarily focused on the health aspects of the crisis, neglecting the economic fallout that millions around the world faced. A more holistic approach is needed to ensure both the health and economic well-being of nations during such crises.

Lastly, criticisms of bias and politicization within the WHO's handling of the pandemic must be addressed. Accusations of favoritism and political influence undermined the organization's credibility and hindered its ability to provide impartial guidance during the crisis. Restoring trust in the WHO requires a thorough examination of these allegations and implementing measures to prevent bias and politicization in the future.

By analyzing the WHO's response to the COVID-19 pandemic, policymakers, diplomats, journalists, educators, and the public can gain valuable insights into the weaknesses that need to be addressed. This analysis serves as a roadmap for improvements in transparency, communication, timely action, collaboration, resource allocation, mental health support, economic mitigation, inclusivity, and impartiality. It is essential to hold the WHO accountable and work towards strengthening international health organizations to better protect global health in the face of future crises.

Chapter 2: Lack of Transparency in Decision-Making Process

The need for transparency in global health emergencies

In the face of a global health emergency such as the COVID-19 pandemic, it is imperative that organizations responsible for handling the crisis prioritize transparency. Transparency not only ensures accountability but also fosters trust and confidence among the public, which is crucial for effective crisis management. Unfortunately, the World Health Organization (WHO) has been heavily criticized for its lack of transparency in its response to the pandemic, which has led to several weaknesses in its handling of the crisis.

One of the major weaknesses of the WHO's COVID-19 response has been the lack of transparency in its decision-making process. Politicians, diplomats, journalists, educators, and the public have expressed concerns about the opacity surrounding key decisions, such as the timing of travel restrictions, the efficacy of certain treatments, and the release of crucial information. The lack of transparency has not only fueled conspiracy theories but has also hindered the public's ability to understand and trust the organization's actions.

Furthermore, inconsistent messaging and communication with the public have been detrimental to the WHO's credibility. The organization's failure to provide clear and concise information, along with contradictory statements from its officials, have created confusion and eroded public trust. This has led to the spread of misinformation and hindered the implementation of preventive measures.

The delayed response and slow action in implementing necessary measures have also been major weaknesses of the WHO's COVID-19 response. The organization's inability to swiftly respond to the emerging crisis allowed the virus to spread rapidly, resulting in severe consequences for public health and global economies. The lack of transparency in decision-making processes and inadequate coordination and collaboration with other international health organizations further exacerbated these delays.

Insufficient allocation of resources and funding has also undermined the WHO's ability to effectively respond to the pandemic. The organization's heavy reliance on voluntary contributions from member states has limited its capacity to address the urgent needs of developing countries and support healthcare systems in dire need of assistance.

Moreover, the WHO's neglect of the mental health impact and economic consequences of the pandemic has drawn significant criticism. The organization's response has primarily focused on public health measures, neglecting the psychological toll on individuals and communities, as well as the economic hardships faced by many.

The limited focus on vulnerable populations and marginalized communities is another area where the WHO's response has been lacking. Critics argue that the organization has not adequately addressed the unique challenges faced by these groups, leading to further health disparities and inequities.

Lastly, criticisms of bias and politicization within the organization's handling of the pandemic have further undermined its credibility. The lack of transparency and perceived biases have fueled skepticism and hindered effective collaboration with member states.

In conclusion, the weaknesses of the WHO's COVID-19 response can largely be attributed to a lack of transparency. The need for transparency in global health emergencies cannot be understated. It is crucial for politicians, diplomats, journalists, educators, and the public to demand transparency from organizations like the WHO to ensure accountability, foster trust, and ultimately improve crisis management. Only through increased transparency can the weaknesses of the WHO's response be addressed and lessons learned for future global health emergencies.

Challenges in accessing timely and accurate information

In the midst of a global crisis such as the COVID-19 pandemic, the importance of timely and accurate information cannot be overstated. However, the World Health Organization (WHO) has faced numerous challenges in providing such information, which has had far-reaching consequences for politicians, diplomats, journalists, educators, and the public.

One of the weaknesses of the WHO's response to the pandemic has been a lack of transparency in the decision-making process. This has made it difficult for stakeholders to understand and trust the organization's actions and recommendations. Without access to the reasoning behind these decisions, politicians and diplomats have struggled to effectively respond to the crisis, while journalists have faced obstacles in providing accurate information to the public.

Inconsistent messaging and communication with the public has further complicated the situation. The WHO's messaging has at times been contradictory or confusing, leading to a lack of clarity and confidence in the organization's guidance. This has made it challenging for educators to convey accurate information to students and for the public to make informed decisions about their health and safety.

Another significant challenge has been the delayed response and slow action in implementing measures. The WHO has been criticized for not acting swiftly enough in declaring a public health emergency and recommending appropriate measures to curb the spread of the virus. This has resulted in the exacerbation of the pandemic and the loss of countless lives.

The failure to effectively coordinate and collaborate with other international health organizations has also hindered the WHO's ability to provide timely and accurate information. By not leveraging the expertise and resources of these organizations, the WHO has missed opportunities to enhance its response and provide more accurate information to the public.

Insufficient allocation of resources and funding has been another obstacle in accessing timely and accurate information. The WHO has faced financial constraints that have limited its capacity to collect, analyze, and disseminate data in a timely manner. This has impeded its ability to provide accurate information to politicians, diplomats, journalists, educators, and the public.

Moreover, the WHO's inadequate support for healthcare systems in developing countries has further exacerbated the challenges in accessing timely and accurate information. These countries often lack the necessary infrastructure and resources to collect and report data effectively, leaving crucial information gaps that hinder the global response to the pandemic.

The mental health impact of the pandemic has been widely recognized, yet the WHO has been criticized for neglecting this aspect in its response. The organization's failure to address the mental health consequences of the pandemic has left individuals and communities without the necessary support and resources to cope with the psychological toll of the crisis.

Furthermore, the WHO has struggled to address and mitigate the economic consequences of the pandemic. Its focus on the health aspects of the crisis has at times overshadowed the need to address the economic hardships faced by individuals, businesses, and communities. This has left many vulnerable populations without the necessary support to navigate the financial challenges brought on by the pandemic.

Lastly, criticisms of bias and politicization within the organization's handling of the pandemic have further hindered access to timely and accurate information. Accusations of favoritism, lack of independence, and political influence have eroded trust in the WHO's ability to provide unbiased information and guidance.

In conclusion, the challenges in accessing timely and accurate information have posed significant obstacles in the WHO's response to the COVID-19 pandemic. The weaknesses identified in the organization's handling of the crisis have impacted politicians, diplomats, journalists, educators, and the public, limiting their ability to make informed decisions and effectively respond to the global health emergency. Addressing these challenges will be crucial in strengthening the global health architecture and ensuring a more effective response to future pandemics.

Criticisms of the World Health Organization's decision-making process

The World Health Organization (WHO) has faced significant criticism regarding its decision-making process in handling the COVID-19 pandemic. This subchapter aims to shed light on the weaknesses of the organization's response, providing an analysis that will be of interest to politicians, diplomats, journalists, educators, and the general public.

One major criticism revolves around the lack of transparency in the WHO's decision-making process. Many have argued that the organization's actions and recommendations have not been adequately explained or justified, leading to confusion and a lack of trust among the public. This lack of transparency has raised concerns about the organization's accountability and its ability to effectively address the pandemic.

In addition, the inconsistent messaging and communication with the public have further eroded trust in the WHO. Mixed messages and conflicting information from the organization have caused confusion and hindered public compliance with recommended measures. Clear and consistent communication is crucial during a crisis, and the WHO's shortcomings in this area have had serious consequences.

Another criticism is the delayed response and slow action in implementing measures. The WHO has been accused of being too slow in recognizing the severity of the pandemic and responding accordingly. This delay has allowed the virus to spread rapidly, resulting in significant loss of life and economic damage.

Furthermore, the WHO has faced criticism for its failure to effectively coordinate and collaborate with other international health organizations. This lack of collaboration has hindered the global response to the pandemic and has impeded efforts to share vital information and resources.

Insufficient allocation of resources and funding has also been a point of contention. The WHO's budget and resources have been criticized as inadequate for effectively addressing the pandemic and supporting healthcare systems in developing countries. This has resulted in a lack of support for healthcare workers and inadequate access to essential medical supplies.

The mental health impact of the pandemic has been largely neglected by the WHO, according to critics. The organization has not prioritized addressing the psychological impact of the crisis, leaving individuals and communities struggling with increased anxiety, depression, and trauma.

Additionally, the WHO has been unable to adequately address and mitigate the economic consequences of the pandemic. Critics argue that the organization's focus has been primarily on the health aspects of the crisis, neglecting the economic impact on businesses, workers, and vulnerable populations.

Moreover, the WHO's limited focus on vulnerable populations and marginalized communities has been a point of concern. Critics argue that the organization should have placed greater emphasis on protecting and supporting these groups, who have been disproportionately affected by the pandemic.

Finally, the WHO has faced accusations of bias and politicization in its handling of the pandemic. Some argue that the organization has been influenced by political interests, compromising its ability to provide objective and evidence-based guidance.

In conclusion, the World Health Organization's decision-making process has been subject to numerous criticisms in its response to the COVID-19 pandemic. Lack of transparency, inconsistent messaging, delayed response, failure to collaborate effectively, insufficient allocation of resources, neglect of mental health and economic consequences, limited focus on vulnerable populations, and accusations of bias and politicization are among the key weaknesses that have been identified. These criticisms highlight the need for reforms and improvements within the organization to ensure a more effective and accountable response to future global health crises.

Chapter 3: Inconsistent Messaging and Communication with the Public

Importance of clear and consistent messaging during a pandemic

In the midst of a global pandemic, clear and consistent messaging is of utmost importance. The World Health Organization (WHO) plays a crucial role in providing guidance and information to the public, policymakers, and healthcare professionals. However, the weaknesses in the organization's handling of the COVID-19 pandemic have highlighted the need for improved communication strategies.

Clear and consistent messaging is vital for several reasons. First and foremost, it helps to establish trust and credibility. In times of crisis, people rely on accurate and reliable information to make informed decisions and take necessary precautions. By providing consistent messaging, the WHO can instill confidence in the public and ensure that they are well-informed about the virus, its transmission, and the recommended preventive measures.

Furthermore, clear messaging helps to avoid confusion and misinformation. Inconsistent or contradictory information can lead to skepticism and distrust, which can have serious consequences during a public health crisis. Politicians, diplomats, journalists, educators, and the public rely on the WHO for accurate and reliable information, and any inconsistencies can undermine their efforts to effectively respond to the pandemic.

Consistent messaging also facilitates effective policy implementation. Policymakers need clear and concise guidelines to develop and implement strategies to combat the spread of the virus. Inconsistent messaging can create confusion among policymakers, leading to delayed response and slow action in implementing necessary measures. This can have dire consequences, as timely and effective action is crucial in containing the spread of the virus and mitigating its impact.

Moreover, clear and consistent messaging is essential for international coordination and collaboration. The WHO must effectively communicate with other international health organizations, governments, and healthcare systems to promote a unified global response. Inconsistent messaging can hinder collaboration efforts and impede the sharing of vital information and resources.

It is also important to acknowledge the diverse needs and vulnerabilities of different populations. Clear and consistent messaging should address the concerns of vulnerable populations and marginalized communities, ensuring that they have access to accurate information and appropriate support. Neglecting these populations can exacerbate existing inequalities and further widen the health disparities.

In conclusion, clear and consistent messaging is crucial during a pandemic. The weaknesses in the WHO's response to the COVID-19 pandemic have highlighted the need for improved communication strategies. By providing accurate, reliable, and consistent information, the WHO can enhance public trust, facilitate effective policy implementation, foster international collaboration, and address the diverse needs of different populations. It is essential for policymakers, diplomats, journalists, educators, and the public to have access to clear and consistent messaging to effectively respond to the challenges posed by the pandemic.

Instances of conflicting information from the World Health Organization

In the midst of the global COVID-19 pandemic, the World Health Organization (WHO) has faced numerous criticisms and challenges in its response. One of the key weaknesses that has emerged is the instances of conflicting information from the organization itself. This subchapter delves into the various instances where the WHO has provided inconsistent messaging and contradictory information, leaving politicians, diplomats, journalists, educators, and the public confused and uncertain.

First and foremost, the lack of transparency in the decision-making process has contributed to the conflicting information from the WHO. The organization's internal discussions and debates on key issues have not been made public, making it difficult to understand the rationale behind their recommendations. This lack of transparency has resulted in a lack of trust in the organization and its guidance.

Moreover, the delayed response and slow action in implementing measures have further exacerbated the issue of conflicting information. As the pandemic rapidly spread across the globe, the WHO's initial response was criticized for being sluggish and inadequate. This delay in taking decisive action has led to contradictory information being disseminated by the organization at different stages of the pandemic.

Furthermore, the failure to effectively coordinate and collaborate with other international health organizations has also contributed to conflicting information. The WHO's role as a global health leader necessitates close collaboration with other organizations such as the Centers for Disease Control and Prevention (CDC) and the European Centre for Disease Prevention and Control (ECDC). However, the lack of coordination has resulted in different organizations providing varying guidelines and recommendations, further adding to the confusion.

In addition, insufficient allocation of resources and funding has hampered the WHO's ability to provide consistent and accurate information. The organization has struggled to keep up with the rapidly evolving nature of the pandemic, leading to contradictory statements and guidance.

Overall, the instances of conflicting information from the WHO have raised serious concerns about its ability to effectively respond to the COVID-19 pandemic. The lack of transparency, inconsistent messaging, delayed response, and failure to collaborate with other organizations have all contributed to a lack of trust and confidence in the organization's handling of the crisis. As politicians, diplomats, journalists, educators, and the public seek reliable and accurate information, it is imperative that the WHO addresses these weaknesses and improves its communication strategies to ensure consistent and reliable guidance in future public health emergencies.

Impact of inconsistent messaging on public trust and response

In the midst of a global crisis such as the COVID-19 pandemic, clear and consistent messaging is crucial for building public trust and facilitating an effective response. Unfortunately, the World Health Organization (WHO) has been plagued by inconsistencies in their messaging, which has had significant implications for public perception and the global fight against the virus.

One of the most detrimental effects of inconsistent messaging is the erosion of public trust. When individuals receive conflicting information from trusted sources, they become confused and uncertain about the appropriate actions to take. This confusion can lead to skepticism and a lack of compliance with public health measures, hindering efforts to control the spread of the virus. Politicians, diplomats, journalists, educators, and the public alike have been affected by this lack of consistent messaging, resulting in a fragmented response to the pandemic.

Moreover, inconsistent messaging can lead to a decrease in public confidence in the WHO itself. As a key international health organization, the WHO plays a critical role in guiding global health responses. However, the organization's inconsistent communication has raised doubts about their ability to effectively lead and manage the pandemic. This loss of confidence can have serious consequences for the organization's credibility and influence, hampering its ability to coordinate and collaborate with other international health organizations and governments.

Furthermore, inconsistent messaging can contribute to misinformation and the spread of conspiracy theories. When the public receives conflicting information, they may turn to alternative sources for guidance, some of which may disseminate false or misleading information. This proliferation of misinformation undermines public health efforts and can exacerbate the impact of the pandemic.

To address these issues, it is imperative that the WHO takes immediate steps to improve the consistency and clarity of its messaging. This includes ensuring that information is based on the best available scientific evidence, regularly updating guidelines and recommendations as new data emerges, and coordinating efforts to align messaging with other international health organizations.

Additionally, the WHO must prioritize transparency and open communication with the public. This includes acknowledging and addressing any mistakes or inconsistencies in their messaging, actively engaging with the concerns and questions of the public, and providing regular updates on the evolving situation.

By strengthening their messaging and rebuilding public trust, the WHO can regain its role as a trusted authority in the global response to the COVID-19 pandemic. However, this will require a concerted effort from the organization, politicians, diplomats, journalists, educators, and the public to prioritize accurate information and effective communication. Only through consistent messaging can we hope to navigate the challenges of this pandemic and protect the health and well-being of all communities, particularly the most vulnerable among us.

Chapter 4: Delayed Response and Slow Action in Implementing Measures

Timeliness as a crucial factor in controlling a pandemic

Introduction:

In the face of a pandemic, timeliness plays a critical role in effectively controlling and mitigating its impact. This subchapter aims to shed light on the significance of timely decision-making, response, and action in combating a global health crisis such as the COVID-19 pandemic. By addressing the weaknesses of the World Health Organization's (WHO) COVID-19 response, including delayed response, inadequate coordination, and insufficient allocation of resources, this subchapter emphasizes the importance of timely measures to save lives and minimize the socio-economic consequences of a pandemic.

Timely Decision-Making and Response:

The timely decision-making process is pivotal in managing a pandemic efficiently. However, the lack of transparency in the WHO's decision-making process has raised concerns among politicians, diplomats, journalists, educators, and the public. By addressing this weakness, the organization can restore trust and ensure that decisions are made with the utmost transparency, taking into account the best available scientific evidence.

Inconsistent Messaging and Communication:

Effective communication with the public is crucial during a pandemic. The WHO has been criticized for inconsistent messaging and communication, leading to confusion and misinformation. By improving communication channels and maintaining consistent messaging, the organization can ensure that accurate information reaches the public promptly, empowering individuals to take appropriate measures to protect themselves and others.

Coordination and Collaboration:

Timely coordination and collaboration with other international health organizations are essential in responding to a pandemic. The failure of the WHO to effectively coordinate and collaborate with other organizations has hindered the global response to COVID-19. By prioritizing collaboration and establishing effective communication channels, the organization can promote timely sharing of information, resources, and expertise, ultimately enhancing global pandemic control efforts.

Allocation of Resources and Funding:

Insufficient allocation of resources and funding has undermined the WHO's ability to respond promptly and adequately to the COVID-19 pandemic. By addressing this weakness and ensuring sufficient resources are allocated, the organization can strengthen its capacity to implement timely measures, provide support to healthcare systems in developing countries, and address the needs of vulnerable populations and marginalized communities.

Conclusion:

Timeliness is an indispensable factor in controlling a pandemic. By addressing the weaknesses of the WHO's COVID-19 response, including delayed response, inadequate coordination, and insufficient resource allocation, the organization can enhance its ability to respond promptly and effectively to future health crises. This subchapter serves as a call to action for politicians, diplomats, journalists, educators, and the public to recognize the importance of timeliness in pandemic control and support efforts to strengthen global health governance. By prioritizing timeliness, transparency, and collaboration, we can improve our collective response to future global health emergencies, ensuring the well-being of humanity as a whole.

Analysis of the World Health Organization's response timeline

The COVID-19 pandemic has exposed various weaknesses in the World Health Organization's (WHO) response, which has prompted the need for a thorough analysis of their actions and decisions. This subchapter aims to provide an in-depth examination of the timeline of the WHO's response to the pandemic, highlighting key moments that have raised concerns among politicians, diplomats, journalists, educators, the public, and various niches.

One of the primary weaknesses identified in the WHO's response is the lack of transparency in their decision-making process. Throughout the timeline, there have been instances where important decisions were made without sufficient explanation or public consultation. This lack of transparency has raised questions about the organization's accountability and the extent to which external influences may have impacted their decision-making.

Another critical aspect is the inconsistent messaging and communication with the public. The WHO's messaging has at times been confusing and contradictory, leading to public confusion and mistrust. Clear and consistent communication is crucial during a crisis, and the WHO's failure to effectively convey information has hindered public understanding and compliance with necessary measures.

A concerning pattern that emerges from the analysis is the delayed response and slow action in implementing measures. The timeline reveals instances where the WHO took an extended period to declare a public health emergency or issue guidelines, which allowed the virus to spread unchecked. This slow response has had severe consequences, contributing to the rapid escalation of the pandemic.

Furthermore, the WHO has faced criticism for its failure to effectively coordinate and collaborate with other international health organizations. The pandemic required a unified global response, but the WHO's coordination efforts have been inadequate, leading to fragmented and disjointed actions by different countries and organizations. This lack of collaboration has hindered the effectiveness of the global response and exacerbated the spread of the virus.

The organization's limited focus on vulnerable populations and marginalized communities is another significant weakness. The pandemic has disproportionately affected these groups, yet the WHO's response has not adequately addressed their specific needs and challenges. This oversight has perpetuated existing health inequalities and widened the gap between different socio-economic groups.

Criticism has also been directed at the WHO for neglecting the mental health impact of the pandemic and failing to address and mitigate the economic consequences. The mental health toll of the pandemic has been substantial, and the WHO's response has largely overlooked this aspect. Additionally, the economic fallout has been severe, but the organization's efforts to support and alleviate the economic burden have been insufficient.

Lastly, there have been criticisms of bias and politicization within the organization's handling of the pandemic. Accusations of favoritism and political influence have cast doubts on the impartiality of the WHO's decision-making process. These allegations have further eroded public trust in the organization and undermined its credibility.

In conclusion, the analysis of the WHO's response timeline reveals several weaknesses in their handling of the COVID-19 pandemic. These weaknesses include the lack of transparency in decision-making, inconsistent messaging, delayed response, inadequate coordination, insufficient resource allocation, neglect of vulnerable populations, disregard for mental health impacts, failure to address economic consequences, limited focus on marginalized communities, and criticisms of bias and politicization. Addressing these weaknesses is crucial for the WHO to regain public trust and strengthen its ability to respond effectively to future global health crises.

Consequences of delayed response and slow action

The consequences of delayed response and slow action in the face of a global pandemic like COVID-19 are far-reaching and can have severe repercussions for individuals, communities, and nations. In this subchapter, we will explore the grave consequences that stem from the World Health Organization's (WHO) inability to promptly address the crisis.

First and foremost, delayed response and slow action in implementing measures to curb the spread of the virus result in a higher rate of infections and deaths. By the time the necessary interventions are put in place, the virus has already gained a significant foothold, making containment efforts more challenging and less effective. This delayed response has cost countless lives and has put immense strain on healthcare systems worldwide.

Furthermore, the economic consequences of a slow response are also dire. Delayed action means that economies are subjected to prolonged lockdowns and restrictions, resulting in widespread job losses, business closures, and economic downturns. Governments are forced to bear the burden of providing financial support to individuals and businesses, leading to increased public debt and long-term economic instability.

The lack of coordination and collaboration with other international health organizations exacerbates the consequences of delayed response. In a global crisis, effective cooperation is crucial to share knowledge, resources, and expertise. The WHO's failure to effectively coordinate with other organizations hampers the collective response to the pandemic, hindering the progress towards finding solutions and mitigating the impact.

Moreover, the insufficient allocation of resources and funding further compounds the consequences. Without adequate resources, healthcare systems struggle to cope with the influx of patients, leading to overwhelmed hospitals, shortages of essential medical supplies, and a diminished quality of care. Developing countries, in particular, face even greater challenges due to limited resources and lack of support from the WHO.

The neglect of the mental health impact of the pandemic is another consequence of delayed response and slow action. The prolonged isolation, fear, and grief experienced during this crisis have taken a toll on individuals' mental well-being. The WHO's failure to address this aspect adequately leaves many vulnerable populations without the necessary support and resources to cope with the psychological impact of the pandemic.

In conclusion, the consequences of delayed response and slow action by the WHO in handling the COVID-19 pandemic are substantial and far-reaching. From increased infections and deaths to economic instability and mental health challenges, the repercussions are felt by individuals, communities, and nations alike. Urgent reforms and improvements are necessary to ensure a more efficient and effective response to future global health crises.

Chapter 5: Failure to Effectively Coordinate and Collaborate with Other International Health Organizations

Importance of collaboration in global health emergencies

In the face of a global health emergency such as the COVID-19 pandemic, collaboration becomes a critical element in mounting an effective response. The weaknesses of the World Health Organization (WHO) in handling the pandemic have highlighted the dire need for improved collaboration among international health organizations, governments, and other stakeholders. This subchapter explores the importance of collaboration in global health emergencies and its potential to address the weaknesses identified in the WHO's COVID-19 response.

Collaboration is crucial in global health emergencies because it brings together diverse expertise, resources, and perspectives. By pooling knowledge and resources, collaboration enhances the ability to understand and respond to complex challenges such as the COVID-19 pandemic. Involving various stakeholders, including politicians, diplomats, journalists, educators, and the public, fosters a multidimensional approach to problem-solving and decision-making.

One of the weaknesses highlighted in the WHO's response was the lack of transparency in the decision-making process. Collaboration can address this by promoting transparency and accountability among all involved parties. By working together, stakeholders can ensure that decision-making processes are transparent, inclusive, and evidence-based, thus fostering public trust.

Inconsistent messaging and communication with the public have also been identified as weaknesses. Collaboration can help overcome this by facilitating coordinated and coherent communication strategies. By working together, stakeholders can ensure that accurate and timely information reaches the public, minimizing confusion and misinformation.

Another weakness identified was the delayed response and slow action in implementing measures. Collaboration can expedite response efforts by streamlining processes, sharing best practices, and coordinating actions. By establishing effective collaboration mechanisms, such as international task forces or joint emergency response teams, stakeholders can act swiftly and decisively, mitigating the impact of the health emergency.

The failure to effectively coordinate and collaborate with other international health organizations is another area of concern. Collaboration can bridge this gap by fostering partnerships and sharing expertise. By leveraging the strengths of different organizations, the collective response can be strengthened, ensuring a more comprehensive and efficient approach.

Insufficient allocation of resources and funding is another weakness. Collaboration can help address this by mobilizing resources from multiple sources and ensuring their effective utilization. By working together, stakeholders can pool their resources, leverage their networks, and advocate for increased funding, thereby strengthening global health systems' capacity to respond.

Collaboration is also vital in addressing and mitigating the economic consequences of the pandemic. By involving economists, policymakers, and financial institutions, stakeholders can develop comprehensive strategies that balance public health measures with economic recovery efforts. By working together, they can ensure that the economic impact is minimized, and support is provided to businesses and individuals affected by the crisis.

Furthermore, collaboration is essential in focusing on vulnerable populations and marginalized communities. By involving educators, healthcare professionals, and community leaders, stakeholders can develop targeted interventions that address the specific needs of these groups. Collaboration can help ensure that no one is left behind in the response efforts, and equity is prioritized.

Lastly, addressing criticisms of bias and politicization within the organization's handling of the pandemic requires collaboration. By involving a diverse range of stakeholders, including journalists, diplomats, and politicians, transparency can be ensured, and decision-making processes can be shielded from undue influence. Collaboration can help build trust and confidence in the response efforts, enhancing the legitimacy and effectiveness of international health organizations.

In conclusion, collaboration plays a crucial role in addressing the weaknesses identified in the WHO's COVID-19 response. By bringing together politicians, diplomats, journalists, educators, and the public, collaboration can enhance transparency, communication, and decision-making processes. It can expedite response efforts, ensure effective coordination, allocate resources efficiently, and address the specific needs of vulnerable populations. Collaboration is essential in mitigating the economic consequences, addressing criticisms of bias and politicization, and fostering a comprehensive and inclusive approach to global health emergencies.

Examination of the World Health Organization's collaboration efforts

The World Health Organization (WHO) has been at the forefront of the global response to the COVID-19 pandemic. However, its collaboration efforts have come under scrutiny, raising concerns about its ability to effectively handle the crisis. This subchapter delves into the weaknesses of the WHO's collaboration efforts, shedding light on the areas that require improvement.

One of the key weaknesses identified is the lack of transparency in the organization's decision-making process. Politicians, diplomats, journalists, educators, and the public have voiced concerns over the opacity of the WHO's decision-making, which has led to a lack of trust and credibility. To effectively address this weakness, the organization must prioritize transparency, ensuring that its decisions and actions are communicated clearly and openly to all stakeholders.

Inconsistent messaging and communication with the public have also been a significant challenge. The WHO must recognize the importance of clear and consistent communication to combat misinformation and ensure that accurate information reaches the public. By improving its messaging strategies, the organization can enhance its credibility and build public trust.

Another weakness lies in the delayed response and slow action in implementing measures. The WHO must work towards swift and decisive action to contain outbreaks and mitigate the spread of the virus. Timely response is crucial in a pandemic situation, and the organization must prioritize quick decision-making and implementation of necessary measures.

Additionally, the WHO has faced criticism for its failure to effectively coordinate and collaborate with other international health organizations. Collaboration is essential in a global crisis, and the organization must strengthen its partnerships and coordination efforts to ensure a unified response.

Insufficient allocation of resources and funding has also hindered the WHO's response. To address this weakness, politicians and policymakers must prioritize funding and resource allocation to support the organization's efforts adequately.

Furthermore, the WHO must address the inadequate support for healthcare systems in developing countries. The pandemic has exposed the vulnerabilities of healthcare systems in these regions, and the organization must work towards providing the necessary support and resources to ensure equitable access to healthcare.

Neglecting the mental health impact of the pandemic is another area of weakness. The WHO must recognize the long-term mental health consequences of the crisis and implement strategies to address and mitigate these impacts.

The organization's ability to address and mitigate the economic consequences of the pandemic has also been called into question. The WHO must work in collaboration with policymakers and economists to develop comprehensive strategies that address the economic fallout of the crisis.

Moreover, the limited focus on vulnerable populations and marginalized communities is a significant weakness. The WHO must ensure that its response efforts are inclusive and address the specific needs of these populations to mitigate the disproportionate impact they face.

Finally, criticisms of bias and politicization within the organization's handling of the pandemic have further eroded public trust. The WHO must work towards depoliticizing its response efforts and prioritize evidence-based decision-making to regain credibility.

In conclusion, the weaknesses in the World Health Organization's collaboration efforts have highlighted the need for improvement. Transparent decision-making, consistent messaging, swift response, effective coordination, adequate allocation of resources, and a focus on vulnerable populations are crucial areas that require attention. By addressing these weaknesses, the WHO can strengthen its response to the COVID-19 pandemic and enhance its ability to handle future global health crises.

Challenges and consequences of insufficient coordination

In the face of a global crisis like the COVID-19 pandemic, effective coordination and collaboration amongst international organizations are paramount. However, the World Health Organization (WHO) has faced significant challenges and consequences due to its insufficient coordination, resulting in a weakened response to the crisis. This subchapter aims to shed light on the various weaknesses and their implications.

One of the primary weaknesses of the WHO's COVID-19 response is the lack of transparency in the decision-making process. This has generated concerns and mistrust among politicians, diplomats, journalists, educators, and the public. Without clear and transparent decision-making, it becomes challenging to garner support and cooperation, hindering the effectiveness of the response.

Inconsistent messaging and communication with the public have further exacerbated the challenges. The WHO's failure to provide clear, concise, and unified information has led to confusion and misinformation among the global population. This lack of coherence in messaging has resulted in public skepticism and decreased compliance with preventive measures, ultimately hampering efforts to contain the virus's spread.

Another critical challenge has been the delayed response and slow action in implementing measures. The WHO's inability to promptly address the escalating crisis has allowed the virus to gain a foothold, leading to widespread transmission and subsequent loss of lives. This delay has been particularly detrimental in countries with weaker healthcare systems, where the consequences have been devastating.

Furthermore, the organization's failure to effectively coordinate and collaborate with other international health organizations has impeded the global response. The absence of a unified approach has led to duplicated efforts, confusion, and inefficiencies. It is crucial for the WHO to establish robust partnerships and foster cooperation to maximize resources and knowledge-sharing.

Insufficient allocation of resources and funding has also hindered the organization's ability to respond effectively. With limited resources, the WHO has struggled to provide adequate support to healthcare systems in developing countries, exacerbating the disparities in access to healthcare and leaving vulnerable populations at even greater risk.

Moreover, the WHO's neglect of the mental health impact of the pandemic has serious consequences. The emotional toll on individuals and communities cannot be overlooked, as it has long-term implications for overall well-being. The organization must prioritize mental health support and incorporate it into their response strategies.

Addressing and mitigating the economic consequences of the pandemic is another critical challenge that the WHO has faced. The organization's limited focus on vulnerable populations and marginalized communities has resulted in an unequal burden of the economic fallout. It is imperative for the WHO to adopt a comprehensive approach that considers the socioeconomic impact of the pandemic and implements measures to alleviate its effects.

Lastly, criticisms of bias and politicization within the organization's handling of the pandemic have further eroded trust in its response. The WHO must work towards greater transparency, independence, and accountability to regain credibility and effectively address the challenges at hand.

In conclusion, the challenges and consequences of insufficient coordination in the WHO's COVID-19 response are far-reaching. From inadequate transparency and inconsistent messaging to delayed action and limited focus on vulnerable populations, these weaknesses have undermined the organization's ability to mount an effective response. Addressing these challenges requires a concerted effort from politicians, diplomats, journalists, educators, and the public to hold the WHO accountable and advocate for necessary reforms. Only through enhanced coordination, transparency, and collaboration can the WHO fulfill its mandate and successfully navigate future global health crises.

Chapter 6: Insufficient Allocation of Resources and Funding

The role of resources and funding in pandemic response

The role of resources and funding in pandemic response is of utmost importance when analyzing the weaknesses of the World Health Organization's (WHO) handling of the COVID-19 pandemic. The allocation of adequate resources and funding is crucial in enabling an effective and efficient response to the crisis, and it is evident that the WHO fell short in this aspect.

One of the major weaknesses observed in the WHO's response was the insufficient allocation of resources and funding. The organization heavily relies on member states' contributions, which can vary significantly in both quantity and timeliness. This lack of reliable and consistent funding hampers the WHO's ability to respond promptly to emergencies and adequately support healthcare systems in developing countries, who are often the most vulnerable.

Insufficient funding not only affects the organization's ability to provide resources such as personal protective equipment, testing kits, and medical supplies to affected countries but also limits their capacity to conduct research, share critical information, and coordinate efforts with other international health organizations. This lack of coordination and collaboration hinders a unified and effective global response, as witnessed during the COVID-19 pandemic.

Moreover, the WHO's inadequate support for healthcare systems in developing countries exacerbates the already existing disparities in access to healthcare. These countries, with limited resources and fragile healthcare infrastructure, struggle to cope with the demands of a pandemic, resulting in a disproportionate impact on their populations.

The WHO should have prioritized and mobilized resources to assist these countries, ensuring that their healthcare systems were adequately equipped to respond to the crisis.

In addition to the physical health impact, the WHO neglected the mental health consequences of the pandemic. The long-term psychological effects on individuals and communities were not addressed adequately, and the organization failed to provide sufficient guidance and support in this aspect. Mental health should have been integrated into pandemic response strategies, recognizing its importance in overall well-being.

Furthermore, the WHO's inability to address and mitigate the economic consequences of the pandemic is another area of weakness. The organization should have played a more significant role in developing strategies to support economies, protect jobs, and alleviate the financial burden on individuals and businesses. By neglecting this aspect, the WHO missed an opportunity to mitigate the far-reaching consequences of the pandemic.

In conclusion, the weaknesses observed in the WHO's handling of the COVID-19 pandemic highlight the crucial role of resources and funding in pandemic response. Insufficient allocation of resources and funding, inadequate support for healthcare systems in developing countries, neglecting mental health impacts, and the failure to address economic consequences all contributed to the organization's shortcomings. It is imperative for policymakers, diplomats, journalists, educators, and the public to recognize these weaknesses and advocate for stronger resource allocation and funding mechanisms to enhance the WHO's ability to respond effectively to future pandemics.

Analysis of the World Health Organization's resource allocation

In order to effectively tackle the COVID-19 pandemic, it is essential to examine the resource allocation strategies of the World Health Organization (WHO). This subchapter aims to shed light on the weaknesses of the WHO's resource allocation, which have hindered the organization's ability to address the global health crisis adequately.

One of the primary weaknesses of the WHO's resource allocation is the insufficient allocation of funding. Despite being the leading global health organization, the WHO has faced chronic underfunding, which has limited its capacity to respond to the pandemic effectively. This lack of adequate financial resources has hindered the organization's ability to provide crucial support to healthcare systems in developing countries, where the impact of the virus has been particularly severe.

Furthermore, the WHO's resource allocation has neglected the mental health impact of the pandemic. The mental health consequences of the crisis have been vast, with individuals experiencing increased stress, anxiety, and depression. However, the WHO has not prioritized mental health support adequately, leaving many vulnerable populations without the necessary resources and services to cope with the psychological toll of the pandemic.

In addition, the organization has failed to address and mitigate the economic consequences of the pandemic. The global economy has been severely impacted by the crisis, with millions of people losing their jobs and businesses facing bankruptcy. The WHO's limited focus on this aspect has left governments and policymakers struggling to find effective solutions to mitigate the economic fallout.

Moreover, the WHO's resource allocation has been criticized for its limited focus on vulnerable populations and marginalized communities. These groups, including the elderly, people with disabilities, and ethnic minorities, have been disproportionately affected by the pandemic.

However, the WHO's allocation of resources has not adequately addressed their specific needs, exacerbating existing inequalities.

Furthermore, there have been criticisms of bias and politicization within the organization's handling of the pandemic. Some argue that the WHO's decision-making process has been influenced by political considerations, compromising the organization's ability to provide impartial and evidence-based guidance. This has raised concerns about the transparency and integrity of the WHO's resource allocation.

In conclusion, the weaknesses in the World Health Organization's resource allocation have impeded its ability to effectively respond to the COVID-19 pandemic. Insufficient funding, neglect of mental health support, inadequate attention to economic consequences, limited focus on vulnerable populations, and criticisms of bias and politicization have all contributed to the organization's shortcomings. Addressing these weaknesses is crucial in order to strengthen the WHO's response to the ongoing global health crisis.

Implications of inadequate resources on the pandemic response

Subchapter: Implications of Inadequate Resources on the Pandemic Response

Introduction:

The COVID-19 pandemic has exposed numerous weaknesses in the World Health Organization's (WHO) response, with inadequate resources being a critical factor hindering effective crisis management. This subchapter explores the implications of insufficient resources and funding on the global response to the pandemic, addressing the concerns of politicians, diplomats, journalists, educators, and the general public.

1. Strained Healthcare Systems in Developing Countries:

One significant implication of inadequate resources is the burden placed on healthcare systems in developing countries. Insufficient funding hampers these nations' ability to expand testing, provide adequate medical supplies, and enhance healthcare infrastructure. As a result, mortality rates skyrocket, exacerbating the impact of the pandemic on vulnerable populations.

2. Ineffective Coordination and Collaboration:

The WHO's limited resources hinder its ability to effectively coordinate and collaborate with other international health organizations. Insufficient funding results in delayed response times and a lack of synchronized efforts, impeding the global fight against the virus. This weakened coordination undermines the effectiveness of measures implemented, leaving room for the virus to spread further.

3. Neglected Mental Health Impact:

Inadequate resources also lead to a neglect of the mental health impact of the pandemic. The WHO's response fails to provide sufficient support and resources for mental health services, leaving individuals vulnerable to anxiety, depression, and other psychological distress. This oversight not only affects individuals but also compromises the overall well-being of communities and societies.

4. Economic Consequences:

The WHO's inability to address and mitigate the economic consequences of the pandemic has far-reaching implications. Insufficient resources hamper the organization's efforts to provide adequate financial support to affected industries, businesses, and individuals. This results in prolonged economic instability that further hinders the recovery process and exacerbates social disparities.

5. Limited Focus on Vulnerable Populations:

Inadequate resources and funding limit the WHO's ability to prioritize vulnerable populations and marginalized communities. The organization's response fails to address the unique challenges faced by these groups, including limited access to healthcare, education, and social support. Consequently, the pandemic disproportionately impacts these communities, perpetuating existing inequalities.

Conclusion:

The implications of inadequate resources on the pandemic response are far-reaching, affecting healthcare systems, coordination efforts, mental health support, economic stability, and the well-being of vulnerable populations. Addressing these weaknesses is crucial for the WHO to regain public trust and improve its pandemic response strategies. Allocating sufficient resources, funding, and support to these areas is paramount to ensure a more effective and equitable global response to future health crises.

Chapter 7: Inadequate Support for Healthcare Systems in Developing Countries

Disparities in healthcare systems and infrastructure

One of the critical weaknesses in the World Health Organization's (WHO) response to the COVID-19 pandemic lies in the disparities present in healthcare systems and infrastructure worldwide. This subchapter aims to shed light on the inequities that have been exposed during this global crisis, and the subsequent consequences on vulnerable populations and marginalized communities.

The COVID-19 pandemic has highlighted the vast differences in healthcare systems across the globe. Developed countries with robust healthcare infrastructure and resources have been able to respond more effectively, with better testing capabilities, access to medical supplies, and advanced healthcare facilities. However, developing nations, already grappling with limited resources and weak healthcare infrastructure, have faced severe challenges in coping with the pandemic. Insufficient allocation of resources and funding to health systems in these countries has resulted in a lack of essential medical supplies, inadequate healthcare facilities, and overwhelmed healthcare workers.

These disparities have had a disproportionate impact on vulnerable populations and marginalized communities. Disadvantaged groups, including the elderly, individuals with pre-existing health conditions, racial and ethnic minorities, and lower socioeconomic groups, have faced increased risks of severe illness and death due to limited access to quality healthcare. Furthermore, the mental health impact of the pandemic has been largely neglected, leaving individuals without the necessary support and resources to cope with the psychological toll the crisis has taken.

The WHO's failure to effectively coordinate and collaborate with other international health organizations has exacerbated these disparities. The lack of a unified global response has hampered efforts to distribute resources equitably and implement effective strategies to combat the pandemic. Inconsistent messaging and communication with the public have further contributed to confusion and mistrust, impeding the adoption of necessary preventive measures.

Moreover, the organization's inability to address and mitigate the economic consequences of the pandemic has widened the gap between developed and developing nations. The economic fallout has disproportionately affected already disadvantaged communities, exacerbating existing social and economic inequalities.

To address these disparities, it is imperative for policymakers, diplomats, educators, and the public to prioritize strengthening healthcare systems and infrastructure, particularly in developing countries. This includes allocating adequate resources and funding, enhancing healthcare facilities, and investing in healthcare workforce capacity. Additionally, there is a need for a more inclusive approach that focuses on vulnerable populations and marginalized communities, ensuring equitable access to healthcare services, testing, and treatment.

In conclusion, the disparities in healthcare systems and infrastructure have laid bare the weaknesses in the WHO's response to the COVID-19 pandemic. It is crucial for all stakeholders to recognize these shortcomings and work towards a more equitable and comprehensive global health response, ensuring that no one is left behind in the face of future health crises.

World Health Organization's efforts in supporting developing countries

One of the weaknesses highlighted in the analysis of the World Health Organization's COVID-19 response is the inadequate support for healthcare systems in developing countries. However, it is important to acknowledge the efforts made by the organization in addressing this issue and providing assistance to these nations.

The World Health Organization (WHO) has been actively involved in supporting developing countries during the COVID-19 pandemic. Recognizing the unique challenges faced by these nations, the organization has implemented several initiatives to strengthen their healthcare systems and ensure an effective response to the crisis.

Firstly, the WHO has been providing technical guidance and expertise to developing countries, particularly in terms of disease surveillance, testing, and contact tracing. Through its extensive network of experts and partnerships, the organization has been assisting countries in building their capacity to detect and respond to COVID-19 cases. This support has been crucial in helping these nations control the spread of the virus and mitigate its impact on their healthcare systems.

Furthermore, the WHO has been actively involved in mobilizing resources and funding for developing countries. Recognizing the financial constraints faced by these nations, the organization has established various funding mechanisms to provide financial assistance for COVID-19 response efforts. This includes the COVID-19 Solidarity Response Fund, which aims to support countries in need of resources to strengthen their healthcare systems and respond effectively to the pandemic.

In addition to financial support, the WHO has also been advocating for equitable access to COVID-19 vaccines and treatments for developing countries. Through initiatives such as the COVAX Facility, the organization has been working to ensure that low-income countries have access to affordable and effective vaccines. This is crucial in preventing further disparities in global health and enabling developing countries to protect their populations and recover from the pandemic.

Overall, while there have been criticisms of the World Health Organization's handling of the COVID-19 pandemic, it is important to recognize its efforts in supporting developing countries. The organization has been actively involved in providing technical guidance, mobilizing resources, and advocating for equitable access to vaccines. These efforts have been crucial in strengthening healthcare systems in developing countries and mitigating the impact of the pandemic on their populations. However, further improvements and collaborations are needed to address the weaknesses identified and ensure a more effective response to future health crises.

Examination of the gaps and limitations in support

In the wake of the COVID-19 pandemic, the World Health Organization (WHO) has faced intense scrutiny for its response. This subchapter, titled "Examination of the Gaps and Limitations in Support," aims to shed light on the weaknesses and shortcomings of the WHO's handling of the crisis. Targeted towards politicians, diplomats, journalists, educators, and the general public, this analysis seeks to provide a comprehensive understanding of the challenges faced by the organization.

One of the key weaknesses identified is the lack of transparency in the decision-making process. Critics argue that important decisions pertaining to the pandemic response were made behind closed doors, leaving the public in the dark. This lack of transparency eroded trust in the organization and hindered effective communication with the public.

Inconsistent messaging and communication with the public also emerged as a significant limitation. The WHO's guidance and recommendations evolved over time, leading to confusion and skepticism among the public. This inconsistency further undermined public confidence in the organization's ability to effectively handle the crisis.

Another critical weakness was the delayed response and slow action in implementing measures. The WHO's initial response to the pandemic was criticized for being sluggish, resulting in missed opportunities to contain the virus. This delayed response had far-reaching consequences and contributed to the rapid spread of COVID-19 worldwide.

Additionally, the WHO failed to effectively coordinate and collaborate with other international health organizations, impeding a unified global response. This lack of coordination hampered efforts to share knowledge, resources, and best practices, ultimately hindering the global fight against the pandemic.

Furthermore, the insufficient allocation of resources and funding posed a significant challenge. The WHO struggled to secure adequate financial support, limiting its ability to respond effectively and provide crucial assistance to countries in need, particularly in developing regions.

Another critical gap was the inadequate support for healthcare systems in developing countries. These nations faced immense challenges in terms of infrastructure, resources, and healthcare capacity. The WHO's failure to address these specific needs further exacerbated the disparities between developed and developing regions, leaving vulnerable populations even more susceptible to the virus.

Moreover, the mental health impact of the pandemic was largely neglected. The WHO's response primarily focused on the physical aspects of the crisis, overlooking the mental health consequences experienced by individuals and communities. This oversight had profound implications for the well-being and resilience of societies affected by the pandemic.

Furthermore, the organization's ability to address and mitigate the economic consequences of the pandemic was limited. The WHO's response primarily centered on public health measures, while failing to adequately address the economic fallout and provide comprehensive solutions to alleviate the burden on businesses and individuals.

Additionally, the WHO faced criticism for its limited focus on vulnerable populations and marginalized communities. The pandemic disproportionately affected these groups, highlighting systemic inequalities and exacerbating existing social disparities. The organization's failure to prioritize these populations further perpetuated these inequities.

Lastly, criticisms of bias and politicization within the organization's handling of the pandemic emerged. The WHO faced allegations of favoring certain countries or political interests, which undermined its credibility and impartiality. These accusations threatened to overshadow the organization's efforts and hinder its ability to effectively respond to the crisis.

In conclusion, this subchapter delves into the weaknesses and limitations of the WHO's COVID-19 response. By examining these gaps, it becomes evident that there is room for improvement in various aspects of the organization's approach. Addressing these weaknesses is crucial not only for the WHO but also for global health security as a whole.

Chapter 8: Neglecting the Mental Health Impact of the Pandemic

Understanding the mental health consequences of a pandemic

The COVID-19 pandemic has not only posed a significant threat to physical health but has also had a profound impact on mental well-being worldwide. As politicians, diplomats, journalists, educators, and the public, it is crucial to grasp the mental health consequences of this global crisis. This subchapter aims to shed light on the weaknesses of the World Health Organization (WHO) in addressing the mental health impact of the pandemic and the implications it has for various populations.

The WHO's response to the COVID-19 pandemic has been marred by a multitude of weaknesses, one of which is neglecting the mental health impact of the crisis. The organization's primary focus has understandably been on controlling the spread of the virus and minimizing the loss of life. However, the mental health implications of the pandemic cannot be overlooked. The prolonged periods of isolation, fear, and uncertainty have led to increased rates of anxiety, depression, and other mental health disorders across all age groups.

Furthermore, the WHO's limited focus on vulnerable populations and marginalized communities has exacerbated the mental health consequences of the pandemic. Individuals from lower socioeconomic backgrounds, frontline healthcare workers, and those with pre-existing mental health conditions have been disproportionately affected. The lack of targeted interventions and support for these groups has resulted in a widening mental health disparity.

In addition to neglecting mental health, the WHO has also failed to effectively address and mitigate the economic consequences of the pandemic. The resulting job losses, financial instability, and poverty have had a significant impact on mental well-being. Without adequate attention to these economic stressors, the mental health consequences of the pandemic are likely to endure long after the virus is contained.

To address these shortcomings, it is imperative that the WHO collaborates with international health organizations, governments, and stakeholders to develop comprehensive mental health strategies. This includes allocating sufficient resources and funding to support mental health services, particularly in developing countries where healthcare systems are already strained.

Moreover, transparency in decision-making processes, consistent messaging, and effective communication with the public are vital to instill confidence and trust in the organization's efforts. By acknowledging and rectifying these weaknesses, the WHO can strengthen its response to the mental health consequences of the pandemic and ensure that no one is left behind.

In conclusion, understanding the mental health consequences of the COVID-19 pandemic is crucial for policymakers, diplomats, journalists, educators, and the public. By recognizing the weaknesses of the WHO's response in addressing mental health, we can work towards a more inclusive and comprehensive approach to support those affected by the pandemic's psychological toll. It is imperative that we prioritize mental health as an integral part of the global response to this crisis and provide the necessary support and resources to mitigate its long-term impact.

World Health Organization's approach to addressing mental health

The COVID-19 pandemic has not only posed a grave threat to physical health but has also had a significant impact on mental well-being worldwide. Recognizing the importance of addressing mental health in the context of the pandemic, the World Health Organization (WHO) has adopted a comprehensive approach to mitigate the mental health impact and ensure the well-being of individuals during these challenging times.

Firstly, the WHO has emphasized the need for awareness and education regarding mental health issues related to the pandemic. By disseminating accurate and reliable information through various channels, including social media, the organization aims to combat the stigma surrounding mental health and promote a better understanding of the challenges individuals may face.

To address the mental health impact, the WHO has provided guidelines and recommendations for governments, healthcare systems, and communities. These guidelines focus on promoting psychological first aid, strengthening mental health services, and integrating mental health into primary healthcare. By providing evidence-based strategies, the organization assists policymakers in implementing effective measures to support individuals experiencing mental health challenges.

Furthermore, the WHO acknowledges the importance of supporting healthcare systems in developing countries, which often face resource constraints. In collaboration with other international health organizations, the WHO aims to strengthen mental health services in these regions, ensuring that vulnerable populations have access to the care they need.

The organization has also recognized the need to address the economic consequences of the pandemic, which can have a profound impact on mental health. By advocating for policies that prioritize economic recovery and job security, the WHO aims to mitigate the stress and anxiety experienced by individuals due to financial instability.

Moreover, the WHO has made efforts to ensure that its response to the pandemic is inclusive and unbiased. Recognizing the disparities faced by marginalized communities, the organization has focused on tailoring its mental health initiatives to meet the specific needs of these populations. By collaborating with local organizations and engaging with community leaders, the WHO aims to ensure that mental health support reaches everyone, regardless of their background or social status.

While the WHO has faced criticism regarding its handling of the pandemic, particularly in terms of decision-making transparency and coordination with other international health organizations, it has made significant strides in addressing the mental health impact. By prioritizing mental health awareness, providing guidelines for policymakers, supporting healthcare systems, and promoting inclusivity, the WHO strives to ensure the well-being of individuals during these unprecedented times.

In conclusion, the World Health Organization's approach to addressing mental health during the COVID-19 pandemic has been comprehensive and multifaceted. By focusing on awareness, education, and support, the organization aims to mitigate the mental health impact and promote the well-being of individuals across the globe. While challenges and criticisms persist, the WHO's efforts in this domain demonstrate its commitment to addressing the wide-ranging consequences of the pandemic.

Criticisms of the organization's response to mental health needs

One of the most significant criticisms leveled against the World Health Organization (WHO) in its response to the COVID-19 pandemic is its failure to adequately address the mental health impact of the crisis. As politicians, diplomats, journalists, educators, and the general public, it is crucial for us to understand the weaknesses of WHO in handling the mental health needs of individuals affected by the pandemic.

Firstly, the organization's lack of transparency in its decision-making process has hindered the implementation of effective mental health strategies. The WHO's failure to provide clear guidelines and protocols for addressing mental health issues during the pandemic has led to confusion and a lack of consistent approaches across different countries. This inconsistency undermines the credibility of the organization and leaves individuals struggling with mental health challenges without the necessary support.

In addition, the inconsistent messaging and communication with the public have further exacerbated the mental health impact of the pandemic. Mixed messages from the WHO, conflicting advice, and changing recommendations have left individuals uncertain and anxious. The organization must improve its communication strategies to provide accurate and timely information, particularly regarding mental health services available and coping mechanisms during these challenging times.

Furthermore, the delayed response and slow action in implementing measures to address mental health needs have been a significant shortcoming of the WHO. The mental health consequences of the pandemic, such as increased rates of anxiety, depression, and substance abuse, have been widely acknowledged, yet the organization has been slow to prioritize and allocate resources for mental health support. This delay has resulted in missed opportunities to mitigate the long-term impact of the crisis on individuals' mental well-being.

Moreover, the WHO's failure to effectively coordinate and collaborate with other international health organizations has hindered the development and implementation of comprehensive mental health strategies. By not leveraging the expertise and resources of other organizations, the WHO has missed out on valuable insights and innovative approaches to addressing mental health challenges during the pandemic.

Lastly, the organization's limited focus on vulnerable populations and marginalized communities has further exacerbated mental health inequalities. The pandemic has disproportionately affected already marginalized groups, including those with pre-existing mental health conditions, frontline healthcare workers, and individuals in low-income countries. The WHO must prioritize the mental health needs of these populations and ensure that resources and support are accessible and tailored to their specific challenges and circumstances.

In conclusion, the World Health Organization's response to mental health needs during the COVID-19 pandemic has been criticized on various fronts. The lack of transparency, inconsistent messaging, delayed response, and insufficient coordination with other organizations have all contributed to the organization's weaknesses in addressing the mental health impact of the crisis. It is imperative for WHO to acknowledge these criticisms and take swift action to rectify these shortcomings to better serve individuals' mental health needs during times of crisis.

Chapter 9: Inability to Address and Mitigate the Economic Consequences of the Pandemic

Economic impact of the COVID-19 pandemic

The COVID-19 pandemic has not only posed a severe threat to public health but has also had a far-reaching economic impact on a global scale. This subchapter delves into the economic consequences of the pandemic and sheds light on the weaknesses of the World Health Organization (WHO) in effectively addressing and mitigating these consequences. The discussion aims to provide insights for politicians, diplomats, journalists, educators, and the public, who are keen on understanding the economic ramifications of the pandemic and the WHO's role in managing them.

One of the weaknesses of the WHO's response to the pandemic has been the lack of transparency in the decision-making process. The public and policymakers need access to accurate and timely information to understand the economic implications of the crisis and make informed decisions. However, the inconsistent messaging and communication from the WHO have hindered effective planning and response at various levels.

Delay in response and slow action in implementing measures have exacerbated the economic impact of the pandemic. The WHO's failure to act swiftly and decisively has led to prolonged lockdowns, business closures, and job losses, resulting in severe economic recessions and financial instability.

Another weakness of the WHO has been its failure to effectively coordinate and collaborate with other international health organizations. The fragmented response and lack of unified efforts have impeded the global economic recovery and exacerbated disparities between countries.

Insufficient allocation of resources and funding has further hindered the economic recovery from the pandemic. The WHO's limited financial support to healthcare systems in developing countries has left them ill-equipped to handle the crisis, leading to increased suffering and economic setbacks.

Furthermore, the neglect of the mental health impact of the pandemic has aggravated the economic consequences. The psychological toll on individuals and communities has resulted in decreased productivity, increased healthcare costs, and long-term economic challenges.

The inability of the WHO to address and mitigate the economic consequences of the pandemic has highlighted a significant weakness in its response strategy. The focus on public health without considering the broader economic implications has led to missed opportunities for effective interventions and support.

Moreover, the limited focus on vulnerable populations and marginalized communities has exacerbated existing inequalities. The economic impact of the pandemic has disproportionately affected these groups, widening the social and economic divide.

Critics have also raised concerns about bias and politicization within the WHO's handling of the pandemic. These allegations have further eroded public trust in the organization and hindered effective collaboration and response efforts.

In conclusion, the economic impact of the COVID-19 pandemic has been profound, and the weaknesses in the WHO's response have exacerbated these consequences. The lack of transparency, inconsistent messaging, delayed response, inadequate coordination, insufficient resources, and neglect of mental health and vulnerable populations have hindered the organization's ability to effectively address the economic ramifications of the crisis. Addressing these weaknesses is crucial for mitigating the economic fallout and ensuring a more resilient and equitable recovery.

World Health Organization's role in mitigating economic consequences

The World Health Organization (WHO) has played a crucial role in addressing the economic consequences of the COVID-19 pandemic. With its extensive global reach and expertise, the organization has been at the forefront of efforts to minimize the impact of the pandemic on economies worldwide.

One of the key strengths of the WHO in mitigating economic consequences is its ability to provide guidance and recommendations to governments and policymakers. Through its regular updates and reports, the WHO has been instrumental in helping countries develop and implement economic measures that protect both public health and economic stability. This has been particularly important in developing countries, where healthcare systems and economies are often more vulnerable.

Additionally, the WHO has actively worked to coordinate and collaborate with other international health organizations, such as the International Monetary Fund and the World Bank, to ensure a comprehensive and unified response to the economic challenges posed by the pandemic. By leveraging the expertise and resources of these organizations, the WHO has been able to mobilize financial aid and support for countries in need, especially those with limited healthcare infrastructure and resources.

Furthermore, the WHO has recognized the importance of addressing the mental health impact of the pandemic on individuals and communities. By advocating for mental health support and resources, the organization has emphasized the need to address the economic consequences of the pandemic holistically. This includes providing guidance on workplace mental health, supporting vulnerable populations, and promoting the well-being of marginalized communities.

It is important to note that the WHO has also acknowledged its weaknesses and areas for improvement. The organization has actively sought to address criticisms of bias and politicization within its handling of the pandemic. By promoting transparency in decision-making processes and ensuring consistent messaging and communication with the public, the WHO aims to regain trust and credibility.

In conclusion, while the WHO has faced valid criticisms regarding its handling of the COVID-19 pandemic, it has also played a crucial role in mitigating the economic consequences. Through its guidance, coordination with other organizations, support for healthcare systems in developing countries, and focus on vulnerable populations, the WHO has demonstrated its commitment to addressing the economic impact of the pandemic. However, ongoing efforts to improve transparency, communication, and resource allocation are crucial for the organization to effectively fulfill its role in mitigating economic consequences in future global health crises.

Analysis of the organization's effectiveness in addressing economic challenges

In the midst of the unprecedented COVID-19 pandemic, the world turned to the World Health Organization (WHO) for leadership and guidance. However, as this subchapter aims to unveil, the organization's effectiveness in addressing economic challenges during this crisis has been called into question. This analysis will shed light on the weaknesses that have hindered the WHO's response, impacting not only the global economy but also the lives of individuals, communities, and nations.

One of the key weaknesses highlighted is the lack of transparency in the decision-making process. The public, politicians, diplomats, journalists, and educators have expressed concerns about the opacity surrounding the WHO's economic strategies and decision-making. This lack of transparency has eroded confidence and hindered the organization's ability to effectively address economic challenges.

Furthermore, inconsistent messaging and communication with the public have created confusion and undermined the WHO's credibility. Clear and consistent communication is crucial in times of crisis, particularly when addressing economic challenges. The organization's failure to provide concise and accurate information has hindered the public's ability to make informed decisions and undermined their trust in the WHO.

Another significant weakness has been the delayed response and slow action in implementing measures. Swift and decisive action is paramount when addressing economic challenges brought about by a crisis of this magnitude. Unfortunately, the WHO's delayed response has allowed economic consequences to escalate, exacerbating the hardships faced by nations and communities.

In addition, the WHO's failure to effectively coordinate and collaborate with other international health organizations has hampered its ability to address economic challenges comprehensively. By neglecting to foster meaningful partnerships and failing to leverage collective expertise, the organization has missed valuable opportunities to mitigate the economic impact of the pandemic.

Insufficient allocation of resources and funding has also undermined the WHO's effectiveness in addressing economic challenges. Inadequate financial support has limited the organization's ability to provide the necessary aid to healthcare systems in developing countries. This neglect has further deepened inequalities and exacerbated the economic consequences of the pandemic for vulnerable populations and marginalized communities.

Furthermore, the WHO's limited focus on the mental health impact of the pandemic has been criticized. The economic challenges brought about by the crisis have had a profound impact on individuals' mental well-being, yet the organization has failed to prioritize mental health in its response, further exacerbating the burden faced by individuals and societies.

Lastly, criticisms of bias and politicization within the organization's handling of the pandemic have further eroded its effectiveness in addressing economic challenges. The perception that political motivations and biases have influenced decision-making processes has undermined the WHO's ability to act independently and effectively address the economic consequences of the pandemic.

In conclusion, the weaknesses unveiled in this analysis demonstrate the extent to which the World Health Organization's effectiveness in addressing economic challenges during the COVID-19 pandemic has been compromised. Lack of transparency, inconsistent messaging, delayed response, insufficient coordination, inadequate resource allocation, neglect of mental health impacts, failure to address economic consequences, limited focus on vulnerable populations, and criticisms of bias and politicization have all played a role in hindering the organization's ability to effectively address economic challenges. It is imperative that these weaknesses be acknowledged and rectified to ensure a more effective response to future crises.

Chapter 10: Limited Focus on Vulnerable Populations and Marginalized Communities

Importance of prioritizing vulnerable populations during a pandemic

In the midst of a global pandemic, it is crucial to prioritize the needs of vulnerable populations. These groups, including the elderly, people with underlying health conditions, low-income individuals, and marginalized communities, are often disproportionately affected by the health and socioeconomic consequences of crises such as the COVID-19 pandemic. As we evaluate the weaknesses in the World Health Organization's (WHO) response to this crisis, it becomes evident that a lack of focus on vulnerable populations has been a significant flaw.

The COVID-19 pandemic has underscored the importance of taking a targeted approach to protect the most vulnerable members of society. By failing to adequately address the unique challenges faced by these populations, the WHO has contributed to the exacerbation of existing health and socioeconomic disparities. It is imperative that politicians, diplomats, journalists, educators, and the public recognize the significance of prioritizing the needs of vulnerable populations in pandemic response strategies.

One of the primary reasons for prioritizing vulnerable populations is the ethical imperative to ensure equitable access to healthcare and resources. By directing attention and resources towards these groups, policymakers can mitigate the disproportionate impact of the pandemic on their health and well-being. Additionally, by addressing the specific needs of vulnerable populations, we can better protect the overall population, as these groups often serve as vectors for the spread of infectious diseases.

Moreover, neglecting vulnerable populations can have severe long-term consequences. Failing to address the mental health impact of the pandemic on these groups can result in increased rates of anxiety, depression, and other psychological disorders. Similarly, inadequate support for healthcare systems in developing countries can lead to a prolonged healthcare crisis that extends beyond the pandemic. Furthermore, the economic consequences of the pandemic are often felt most acutely by vulnerable populations, exacerbating existing inequalities and deepening poverty levels.

In order to rectify the weaknesses in the WHO's response to the COVID-19 pandemic, it is essential to prioritize vulnerable populations. This includes ensuring equitable access to healthcare, providing targeted support for mental health services, and creating economic policies that address the specific needs of marginalized communities. By doing so, we can build a more resilient and inclusive society that is better prepared to face future crises. It is the responsibility of politicians, diplomats, journalists, educators, and the public to advocate for the prioritization of vulnerable populations and hold international organizations accountable for their response to the pandemic. Only through collective action can we address the weaknesses in the WHO's handling of the COVID-19 crisis and pave the way for a more equitable and effective global health response.

World Health Organization's approach to addressing the needs of vulnerable communities

In the wake of the COVID-19 pandemic, it has become increasingly evident that vulnerable communities require special attention and support. The World Health Organization (WHO) recognizes the importance of addressing the unique needs of these communities and has implemented several strategies to ensure their well-being during these challenging times.

First and foremost, the WHO has taken steps to increase transparency in its decision-making processes. Recognizing the criticism it faced for lack of transparency, the organization has made efforts to involve diverse stakeholders in its decision-making bodies, including politicians, diplomats, journalists, educators, and the public. This inclusive approach ensures that decisions are made with a wide range of perspectives, making the process more transparent and accountable.

Furthermore, the WHO acknowledges the importance of consistent messaging and communication with the public. To address the criticism of inconsistent messaging, the organization has developed clear guidelines and protocols for disseminating information about COVID-19. These guidelines serve as a framework for member states to communicate effectively with their populations, ensuring that accurate and timely information reaches the public.

The WHO has also recognized the need for a prompt response and swift action in implementing measures to control the spread of the virus. To address the criticism of delayed response, the organization has established an Emergency Response Framework that enables it to rapidly mobilize resources and coordinate with member states. This framework ensures that measures are implemented promptly and effectively, reducing the impact of the pandemic on vulnerable communities.

Additionally, the WHO has made efforts to enhance collaboration with other international health organizations. Recognizing the criticism of failure to effectively coordinate, the WHO has strengthened partnerships with organizations such as the Centers for Disease Control and Prevention (CDC) and the World Bank. These collaborations facilitate the exchange of knowledge, resources, and expertise, enabling a more coordinated and effective response to the pandemic.

The WHO also acknowledges the importance of allocating sufficient resources and funding to address the needs of vulnerable communities.

To address the criticism of insufficient allocation of resources, the organization has advocated for increased funding from member states and international organizations. These funds are used to support healthcare systems in developing countries, provide necessary medical supplies, and promote equitable access to healthcare services.

Furthermore, the WHO recognizes the mental health impact of the pandemic and has taken steps to address this issue. To address the criticism of neglecting mental health, the organization has developed guidelines and resources to support mental well-being during the pandemic. These resources provide guidance on managing stress, anxiety, and grief, ensuring that the mental health needs of vulnerable communities are not overlooked.

In addition, the WHO acknowledges the economic consequences of the pandemic and has implemented measures to mitigate them. To address the criticism of inability to address economic consequences, the organization has advocated for economic stimulus packages, job protection measures, and support for businesses. These efforts aim to alleviate the financial burden on vulnerable communities and promote economic recovery.

Moreover, the WHO recognizes the importance of focusing on vulnerable populations and marginalized communities. To address the criticism of limited focus, the organization has prioritized equity and inclusivity in its response to the pandemic. It has developed guidelines to ensure that the specific needs of vulnerable populations are met, including access to healthcare, social support, and protection from discrimination.

Lastly, the WHO acknowledges the criticisms of bias and politicization within its handling of the pandemic. To address these concerns, the organization has committed to upholding its core values of impartiality, independence, and integrity. It has implemented measures to ensure that its response is guided by evidence-based recommendations and scientific expertise, rather than political considerations.

In conclusion, the WHO has taken significant steps to address the needs of vulnerable communities during the COVID-19 pandemic. Through increased transparency, consistent messaging, prompt response, enhanced collaboration, sufficient allocation of resources, support for healthcare systems, focus on mental health, mitigation of economic consequences, and prioritization of vulnerable populations, the organization has demonstrated its commitment to protecting the most vulnerable members of society. However, continuous evaluation and improvement of these efforts are necessary to ensure that the WHO effectively addresses the weaknesses highlighted during this crisis.

Criticisms of the organization's limited focus in this area

One of the key criticisms aimed at the World Health Organization's (WHO) response to the COVID-19 pandemic has been its limited focus in certain areas. While the organization has played a pivotal role in coordinating global efforts and providing guidance, there are concerns that it has not adequately addressed several crucial aspects of the crisis.

One significant weakness lies in the WHO's failure to effectively prioritize and address the needs of vulnerable populations and marginalized communities. The pandemic has disproportionately affected these groups, exacerbating existing inequalities and amplifying the challenges they face. Critics argue that the organization should have taken a more proactive approach to ensure that these communities received the necessary support and resources to weather the storm. By neglecting their unique needs, the WHO risks perpetuating systemic injustices and exacerbating health disparities.

Another area of concern is the organization's limited attention to the mental health impact of the pandemic. The crisis has taken a toll on people's mental well-being, leading to increased stress, anxiety, and depression. Unfortunately, the WHO's response has been perceived as insufficient, with critics arguing that it should have prioritized mental health support and implemented strategies to address the psychological consequences of the pandemic. By neglecting this aspect, the organization may undermine the overall resilience and recovery of communities affected by COVID-19.

In addition, there have been criticisms of bias and politicization within the organization's handling of the pandemic. Some argue that the WHO's decisions and recommendations have been influenced by political considerations, which can undermine the organization's credibility and independence. To maintain public trust, it is crucial for the WHO to address these concerns and ensure that its response is driven solely by scientific evidence and public health expertise.

For a comprehensive and effective response to a crisis of this magnitude, the WHO must address these criticisms and expand its focus. It should work towards greater transparency in decision-making processes, ensuring consistent and clear communication with the public, and timely implementation of measures. The organization must also strengthen coordination and collaboration with other international health organizations to leverage their expertise and resources. Adequate allocation of funding and resources, coupled with support for healthcare systems in developing countries, is essential to ensure an equitable and sustainable response.

By acknowledging and rectifying these weaknesses, the WHO can strengthen its response to the COVID-19 pandemic and enhance its ability to protect global public health in future crises.

Chapter 11: Criticisms of Bias and Politicization within the Organization's Handling of the Pandemic

Concerns over impartiality and objectivity in the World Health Organization's response

Concerns over impartiality and objectivity in the World Health Organization's (WHO) response to the COVID-19 pandemic have raised significant questions about the organization's ability to effectively tackle global health crises. This subchapter delves into the various criticisms and allegations that have been leveled against the WHO, shedding light on the weaknesses in its approach.

One of the primary concerns surrounding the WHO's response is the lack of transparency in its decision-making process. Critics argue that important decisions regarding public health measures and guidelines were made behind closed doors, without adequate input from independent experts or public scrutiny. This lack of transparency has eroded public trust and confidence in the organization's ability to provide impartial and objective advice.

Furthermore, the WHO has been criticized for inconsistent messaging and communication with the public. As the pandemic unfolded, the organization's guidance and recommendations seemed to change frequently, leading to confusion and mistrust among the general population. This inconsistency has undermined the WHO's credibility and hindered its ability to effectively communicate vital information to the public.

Another key weakness in the WHO's response has been the delayed response and slow action in implementing measures. Critics argue that the organization was slow to declare the COVID-19 outbreak a global health emergency and failed to take swift action to curb the spread of the virus. This delayed response resulted in a rapid escalation of cases and deaths, further exacerbating the global impact of the pandemic.

The WHO's failure to effectively coordinate and collaborate with other international health organizations has also come under scrutiny. Critics argue that the organization was unable to forge strong partnerships and leverage resources from other agencies, leading to a fragmented and disjointed response to the pandemic. This lack of coordination has hindered the global effort to combat the virus and mitigate its impact.

Furthermore, the WHO has been criticized for its insufficient allocation of resources and funding. As the pandemic spread, the organization struggled to mobilize the necessary resources to support healthcare systems in developing countries. This lack of support has further exacerbated the inequalities in global health and left vulnerable populations without adequate care and protection.

The WHO's neglect of the mental health impact of the pandemic and its inability to address and mitigate the economic consequences have also been subject to criticism. Critics argue that the organization's focus on the medical aspects of the pandemic has overshadowed the mental health toll and economic devastation it has caused, leaving individuals and communities without the necessary support and resources.

Lastly, concerns over bias and politicization within the WHO's handling of the pandemic have further undermined its impartiality and objectivity. Allegations of political interference and favoritism have eroded public confidence in the organization's ability to provide independent and evidence-based guidance.

In conclusion, the concerns over impartiality and objectivity in the WHO's response to the COVID-19 pandemic have highlighted significant weaknesses in the organization's handling of the crisis. From lack of transparency in decision-making to inconsistent messaging, delayed response, and failure to effectively coordinate with other international health organizations, these weaknesses have had far-reaching consequences on the global response to the pandemic. It is imperative for the WHO to address these concerns and rebuild public trust to effectively tackle future health crises.

Analysis of instances of bias and politicization

One of the critical areas of concern surrounding the World Health Organization's (WHO) response to the COVID-19 pandemic is the alleged bias and politicization within the organization's decision-making process. This subchapter aims to delve into the analysis of instances where bias and politicization may have influenced the WHO's handling of the pandemic.

From the outset, it is essential to acknowledge that the WHO operates in a complex and politically charged environment. As an international organization, it must navigate the interests and agendas of its member states. However, concerns have been raised regarding the extent to which political considerations have influenced the WHO's response.

One notable criticism is the lack of transparency in the decision-making process. It has been argued that certain decisions made by the WHO, such as the timing and extent of travel restrictions, may have been influenced by political considerations rather than purely scientific evidence. This lack of transparency erodes public trust and hinders effective decision-making.

Furthermore, inconsistent messaging and communication with the public have also been identified as potential instances of bias. The WHO's guidance and recommendations have sometimes been contradictory, leading to confusion and misinformation among the public. This inconsistency may stem from political pressures or the organization's desire to maintain diplomatic relationships.

Another area of concern is the alleged delayed response and slow action in implementing measures. Critics argue that the WHO's reluctance to declare the pandemic a public health emergency of international concern promptly may have been influenced by political factors, leading to a delayed global response and a higher number of COVID-19 cases.

In addition, the WHO's failure to effectively coordinate and collaborate with other international health organizations has raised eyebrows. The organization's ability to work collaboratively with partners is essential in combating a global crisis like COVID-19. Any politicization or bias in these collaborations can hinder the collective effort to mitigate the impact of the pandemic.

It is crucial to address these criticisms and ensure that the WHO remains an impartial and trusted source of information. Transparency in decision-making, consistent messaging, and prompt action are vital in restoring public trust. The organization should prioritize scientific evidence over political considerations to effectively combat future pandemics.

In conclusion, the analysis of instances of bias and politicization within the WHO's handling of the COVID-19 pandemic is critical in assessing the weaknesses of the organization. Addressing these concerns is necessary to restore public trust and ensure that the WHO can effectively fulfill its mandate to protect global health. By acknowledging these weaknesses and working towards rectifying them, the WHO can strengthen its response to future global health crises.

Consequences of perceived bias on public trust and international cooperation

In the complex and interconnected world of global health, the World Health Organization (WHO) plays a crucial role in coordinating international efforts and ensuring effective responses to public health crises. However, the weaknesses exhibited by the organization in its handling of the COVID-19 pandemic have had wide-ranging consequences on public trust and international cooperation.

One of the most significant consequences of perceived bias within the WHO is the erosion of public trust. The lack of transparency in the decision-making process, inconsistent messaging, and delayed response have left the public questioning the credibility and reliability of the organization. This loss of trust not only undermines the effectiveness of public health measures but also hampers the willingness of individuals to comply with guidelines and recommendations.

Moreover, the perception of bias and politicization within the WHO has had a detrimental impact on international cooperation. The organization's failure to effectively coordinate and collaborate with other international health organizations has led to fragmented and disjointed responses to the pandemic. This lack of unity and coordination has hindered the sharing of critical information, resources, and expertise, thereby impeding the global fight against COVID-19.

The consequences of bias within the WHO also extend to the allocation of resources and funding. Insufficient allocation of resources and funding has resulted in a lack of support for healthcare systems in developing countries, exacerbating the inequalities in access to healthcare. This neglect of vulnerable populations and marginalized communities not only perpetuates existing health disparities but also undermines efforts to control the spread of the virus.

In addition, the organization's limited focus on the mental health impact of the pandemic and its inability to address and mitigate the economic consequences further highlight the consequences of perceived bias. By neglecting these crucial aspects, the WHO fails to provide comprehensive and holistic responses to the pandemic, leaving individuals and communities vulnerable to long-term psychological and socio-economic repercussions.

To rebuild public trust and enhance international cooperation, it is imperative for the WHO to address the criticisms of bias and politicization within its handling of the pandemic. The organization must prioritize transparency, consistent messaging, and timely responses in its decision-making process. It should actively engage and collaborate with other international health organizations to ensure a united front against the virus. Additionally, the WHO must allocate sufficient resources and funding to support healthcare systems in developing countries and focus on addressing the needs of vulnerable populations and marginalized communities.

By acknowledging and rectifying its weaknesses, the WHO can regain public trust, strengthen international cooperation, and effectively mitigate the consequences of the COVID-19 pandemic. Only through a concerted global effort can we overcome the challenges posed by this unprecedented health crisis and build a more resilient and equitable world.

Chapter 12: Conclusion

Summary of weaknesses identified in the World Health Organization's COVID-19 response

In the book "Unveiling the Weaknesses: An Analysis of the World Health Organization's COVID-19 Response," several weaknesses in the World Health Organization's handling of the COVID-19 pandemic are highlighted. This subchapter aims to provide a summary of these weaknesses, addressing an audience of politicians, diplomats, journalists, educators, the public, and individuals interested in understanding the flaws in the WHO's response.

Firstly, one major weakness identified is the lack of transparency in the decision-making process. The book points out that important decisions regarding the pandemic response were often made behind closed doors, leading to skepticism and mistrust among the public. This lack of transparency hindered the organization's ability to gain public confidence and effectively manage the crisis.

Another weakness identified is the inconsistent messaging and communication with the public. The book argues that the WHO's messages often changed or contradicted each other, causing confusion and undermining public trust. Clear and consistent communication is crucial during a crisis, and the organization's failure in this aspect resulted in a loss of credibility.

The delayed response and slow action in implementing measures is also highlighted as a weakness. The book argues that the WHO took too long to acknowledge the severity of the pandemic and implement necessary measures. This delayed response allowed the virus to spread rapidly, leading to increased infections and fatalities.

Furthermore, the book criticizes the WHO for its failure to effectively coordinate and collaborate with other international health organizations. The lack of coordination resulted in a fragmented response and limited sharing of crucial information and resources, hindering the global effort to combat the pandemic.

Insufficient allocation of resources and funding is another weakness identified. The book argues that the WHO's response was hindered by a lack of adequate resources and funding, limiting its ability to effectively respond to the crisis and support healthcare systems in developing countries.

The book also points out the inadequate support for healthcare systems in developing countries as a weakness. The WHO's focus on resource-rich countries left many developing nations struggling to cope with the pandemic, exacerbating the global health inequities.

Additionally, the organization's neglect of the mental health impact of the pandemic is highlighted as a weakness. The book argues that the WHO did not prioritize mental health support, despite the significant psychological toll of the crisis on individuals and communities.

The inability to address and mitigate the economic consequences of the pandemic is another weakness identified. The book argues that the WHO's response did not adequately consider the economic impact of the pandemic, leading to further hardships for individuals and economies worldwide.

Moreover, the book criticizes the limited focus on vulnerable populations and marginalized communities. The WHO's response, according to the book, did not sufficiently address the unique challenges faced by these populations, further exacerbating health disparities and inequalities.

Finally, the book raises concerns about bias and politicization within the organization's handling of the pandemic. The WHO's response, as argued in the book, was influenced by political considerations, compromising its ability to provide impartial guidance and support during the crisis.

In conclusion, "Unveiling the Weaknesses: An Analysis of the World Health Organization's COVID-19 Response" highlights several weaknesses in the WHO's response to the pandemic. These weaknesses include a lack of transparency, inconsistent messaging, delayed response, inadequate coordination, insufficient resources, neglect of mental health, inability to address economic consequences, limited focus on vulnerable populations, and criticisms of bias and politicization. Understanding these weaknesses is crucial for policymakers, diplomats, journalists, educators, and the public to advocate for necessary reforms and improvements in global health governance.

Recommendations for improving future global health emergency responses

In light of the weaknesses uncovered in the World Health Organization's (WHO) response to the COVID-19 pandemic, it is crucial to outline key recommendations that can enhance future global health emergency responses. These recommendations are aimed at addressing the concerns raised by politicians, diplomats, journalists, educators, the public, and various niches, including:

1. Enhancing transparency: The WHO should ensure a transparent decision-making process by proactively sharing information, data, and evidence-based research with the public. This would foster trust and enable policymakers to make informed decisions.

2. Clear and consistent communication: The WHO needs to develop a robust communication strategy that ensures consistent messaging to the

public. This includes timely updates, accurate information, and effective use of social media platforms to combat misinformation and confusion.

3. Swift response and decisive action: The WHO should establish protocols for rapid response and implement measures promptly. This involves developing early warning systems, coordinating with member states, and swiftly deploying resources to contain and mitigate the impact of future health emergencies.

4. Strengthening collaboration: The WHO must prioritize effective coordination and collaboration with other international health organizations, such as the Centers for Disease Control and Prevention (CDC) and the World Bank. This collaboration should focus on sharing best practices, pooling resources, and collectively responding to global health crises.

5. Adequate allocation of resources: The international community should commit to increasing funding for the WHO to ensure sufficient resources for pandemic preparedness and response. This includes investing in research and development, strengthening healthcare infrastructure, and supporting the training of healthcare professionals.

6. Support for developing countries: The WHO should prioritize providing technical assistance, capacity-building, and financial support to healthcare systems in developing countries. This would help bridge the existing healthcare disparities and ensure equitable access to healthcare during global health emergencies.

7. Addressing mental health impacts: The WHO should integrate mental health support into emergency response plans, recognizing the long-term psychological consequences of pandemics. This includes training healthcare workers, raising awareness, and providing accessible mental health services for affected individuals.

8. Mitigating economic consequences: The WHO should work closely with international financial institutions to develop comprehensive strategies that address the economic consequences of pandemics. This involves providing financial assistance, supporting job retention programs, and facilitating economic recovery for affected communities.

9. Focus on vulnerable populations: The WHO should prioritize the needs of vulnerable populations and marginalized communities in emergency response plans. This includes tailoring interventions, ensuring access to healthcare services, and addressing social determinants of health to reduce disparities in health outcomes.

10. Addressing bias and politicization: The WHO should establish robust mechanisms to ensure impartiality, transparency, and independence in its decision-making processes. This includes strengthening governance structures, fostering a culture of accountability, and actively addressing any criticisms or allegations of bias and politicization.

By implementing these recommendations, the WHO can strengthen its response to future global health emergencies, rebuild trust, and ensure a more effective and equitable global health system. It is crucial for policymakers, diplomats, journalists, educators, and the public to advocate for these reforms and hold the WHO accountable for their implementation. Only through collective efforts can we prevent and mitigate the devastating impact of future pandemics.

Importance of addressing weaknesses for global health security

In the midst of the COVID-19 pandemic, it has become glaringly clear that the weaknesses within the World Health Organization's (WHO) response have had a profound impact on global health security. Addressing these weaknesses is of utmost importance, not only for the future containment and management of the current pandemic but also for safeguarding global health in the long run. This subchapter aims to shed light on the significance of addressing these weaknesses and the implications they hold for politicians, diplomats, journalists, educators, the public, and various niches.

The weaknesses of the World Health Organization in handling the COVID-19 pandemic have been manifold. The lack of transparency in the decision-making process has eroded public trust and hindered effective communication. Inconsistent messaging and communication with the public have led to confusion and misinformation, thereby undermining public health measures. Delayed response and slow action in implementing measures have allowed the virus to spread and exacerbate its impact on societies.

Furthermore, the failure to effectively coordinate and collaborate with other international health organizations has hampered collective efforts and hindered the sharing of vital information. Insufficient allocation of resources and funding has strained healthcare systems, especially in developing countries, exacerbating the impact of the pandemic. The neglect of the mental health impact and economic consequences of the pandemic has further compounded the crisis.

Addressing these weaknesses is crucial for global health security. By enhancing transparency in decision-making processes, the WHO can rebuild public trust and ensure the dissemination of accurate information. Consistent messaging and communication will help in combating misinformation and promoting effective public health measures. Prompt response and actions are vital to prevent the further spread of the virus and mitigate its impact.

Effective coordination and collaboration with other international health organizations will facilitate the sharing of resources, expertise, and knowledge to effectively combat the pandemic. Adequate allocation of resources and funding will help strengthen healthcare systems and ensure their resilience in the face of future health crises. Recognizing and addressing the mental health impact and economic consequences of the pandemic will help in providing holistic support to affected individuals and communities.

Furthermore, a focus on vulnerable populations and marginalized communities is essential to ensure equitable access to healthcare and mitigate the disproportionate impact of the pandemic on these groups. Addressing criticisms of bias and politicization within the organization's handling of the pandemic is necessary to restore the credibility and integrity of the WHO.

In conclusion, addressing the weaknesses within the World Health Organization's response to the COVID-19 pandemic is of paramount importance for global health security. By acknowledging and rectifying these weaknesses, politicians, diplomats, journalists, educators, the public, and various niches can contribute to a more effective and resilient global health system that can better respond to future health crises. It is imperative that we learn from the lessons of this pandemic to prevent and mitigate the impact of future global health emergencies.